CLEAR WRITTEN COMMUNICATION

Simple tips for getting your message across

Written by Florence Schandeler
Translated by Carly Probert

Coaching 50MINUTES.com

HOW TO BE CLEAR IN YOUR WRITTEN COMMUNICATION

- **Problem:** How can I communicate effectively in writing in order to convey information and make myself better understood?
- **Uses:** Formulating ideas or communicating the results of research in a clear and effective manner. Improving the internal and external communication of your business.
- **Professional context:** Communication, professional relationships, writing skills.
- **FAQs:**
  - How can I fight my writer's block?
  - What types of written communication are found in business?
  - How can I define the purpose of my text?
  - How can I ensure my document contains all the necessary information?
  - How do I formulate an argument?
  - How can I highlight the key ideas of my text?
  - Why should I be concise in my writing and how is this done?
  - What reference tools are used for writing?
  - How can I proofread my document effectively?

"A well-conceived idea is expressed clearly, and the words to say it with arrive with ease" – this mantra has been repeated in chorus by philologists and humanities professors quoting Nicolas Boileau (French writer, 1636-1711). Yet, it is clear that words often fail us when we set about writing our ideas down on paper. Writer's block is not a new phenomenon and does not only affect writers. While writing a report or an e-mail is not exactly an art, it is still a rigorous exercise that requires concentration and practice.

In this booklet, we will teach you how to perfect the ins and outs of written communication, in order to concentrate on its objectives and methods. We will discuss the issues and complexity of writing, the difficulty of embarking on a writing task and we will also present concrete tools for structuring your texts and conveying your ideas effectively.

GOOD WRITING: THE BASICS

Transmitting a message

Roman Jakobson (Russian linguist, 1896-1982) established a diagram showing the components involved in any act of communication.

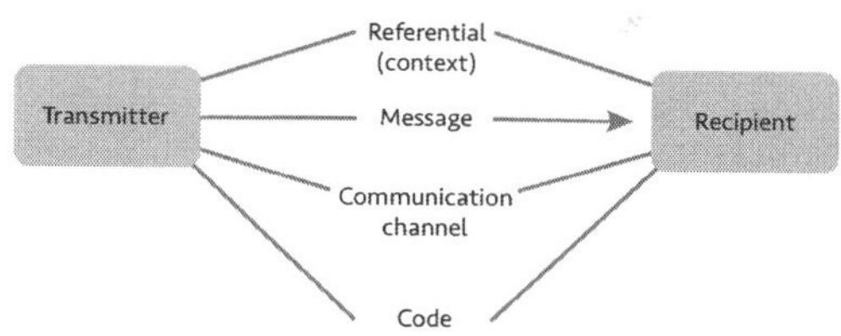

Written Communication © 50MINUTES.com

- **The message** is the subject of the communication, which is transmitted by the transmitter to the receiver.
- **The transmitter** is the person sending the message.
- **The receiver** is the person to whom the message is delivered.
- **The communication channel** is the channel through which the message is delivered (our senses: hearing, sight, etc.).
- **The code** is defined as the set of signs and rules that allow for the efficient production and transmission of

messages. In our case, it is the English language. Other types of code are, for example, the Highway Code or sign language. To understand, the transmitter and the receiver must share a common code.

- **The referent** is the tangible face of the communication. This is the context in which the message is issued. It consists of real objects, the location, the people, etc.

According to the Jakobson diagram, several parameters must be taken into account when transmitting a message. Firstly, so that the receiver is listening, both the transmitter and the receiver must want to communicate with one another: the first encodes the message, while the second decodes it. Then, for the message to be understood, they must both use the same code, i.e. speak the same language and know the words and expression used.

Challenges and pitfalls of written communication

In written communication, the transmitter and the recipient are not necessarily in each other's direct presence. Therefore, this eliminates non-verbal communication (or body language), which is involved in the oral transmission of the message through gestures and intonations. Therefore, the recipient of a written message does not instantly perceive the humorous or ironic character of a subject. Only words convey the message, and therefore acquire considerable importance: they must be accurate enough to communicate a message that is sufficient in itself. Writing requires the transmitter to be clear and direct in their communication and leaves no room for mistakes.

Writing clear and productive business documents is an important asset for you and your business. This skill can help you to:

- improve internal and external communication within the company;
- improve efficiency, which corresponds to the saving of time and money;
- guarantee customer loyalty. If your texts, as a reflection of your business, seem understandable and clear, the customer will be more likely to trust you.

Adapting to the reader

We have already seen that in order to communicate, you need to share the same code and speak the same language, both literally and figuratively; for example, a doctor's language is not the same as that of his patient, therefore he must popularise his dialogue. Social environment, culture, education and our professional lives determine how we express ourselves and our vocabulary. To communicate effectively, we must first ensure that we are understood.

This advice applies to all business documents, be it an e-mail, a report, a prospectus or the minutes of a meeting: constantly imagine yourself in the shoes of the recipient before starting to write. If you are talking to someone who has different technical knowledge from your own, be sure to adjust your vocabulary. If they have to resort to a dictionary several times to decode your message, this is likely to discourage them and they may not understand you completely. For example, if a memo is addressed to all employees of the same company, the transmitter should ensure it is written according to the jargon of the industry. However, if the same transmitter prepares a prospectus or brochure for prospective customers, they should adapt the vocabulary used in order to reach the uninitiated audience.

Which medium to use for which purpose?

Appeals, promotional flyers, minutes from a meeting, a work e-mail, etc. are all written in different forms, and also differ greatly in their purpose: to persuade, inform or make a request. Before determining which media to use, set your communication objective. Therefore, if you want to disseminate information within your company, an informative note or e-mail will work, provided you are thorough in your explanation. If you wish to inform the public of an event happening in your business, choose a prospectus or press release. Also, if your goal is to convince a client, use a business letter and construct good arguments; if you are teaching, provide full explanations.

In all these cases, once the text is written, review your writing to make sure that you have fulfilled your communication objectives.

DARING TO DIVE IN

Preparation

It is not enough to simply sit at your computer and get to work. Preparatory work is required to determine and define the subject to be dealt with and the purpose of your document: what information do you need to transmit? To whom? Why? What is the purpose? Answer these questions on a piece of paper and keep it in front of you while writing.

For certain types of writing, you may need to read up on the subject. If you have not yet chosen an approach, review existing documentation using an internet search engine or search in a university library, for example. During your research, make notes on ideas that seem interesting and summarise them. This information from various sources will provide you with possible starting points on the material. You can also use the pre-writing methods explained below.

subject you want to discuss, without censoring or structuring your thinking. This method has the advantage of focusing your concentration on the task at hand and keeping a written record or all your ideas. You can organise them later in your writing.

- **Mind mapping:** This mapping technique is used to represent your thought process. Working associatively, the idea is to note the keywords – related to your subject – that come to mind or that you discover during your research on a sheet of paper. One idea leads to another, by association, and you may be tempted to explore and deal with other themes and concepts related to your original subject.

Where to start?

Take the time to analyse the main ideas in order to determine the different components that will make up your writing. At this point, the information can be organised in order to highlight the main ideas and then arrange the subtopics. Structure your thoughts with titles and subtitles, if necessary. Do this for any professional writing: e-mails, business letters, notes, minutes, etc.

Once the plan of your text has been defined, it should resemble a shelf that is methodically storing your data. You can then process and classify the information you have previously identified point by point. The choice of your plan (analytical, comparative or otherwise) depends mainly on the purpose of communication and the type of information to be transmitted. Use a comparative plan in the context of a confrontation between two differing views: for example, are you for or against a change to office hours? What are the advantages and disadvantages? Compare the two opinions in a table so that readers are aware of all the information and can select the most appropriate option. If you want to list the decisions resulting from a meeting, is the minutes are more relevant. You can reconsider actions to be taken and arrangements for each of these (the people involved, objectives, place and date).

STRUCTURE AND WRITING

Devising a clear and coherent plan

A text, whether professional or not, generally has a ternary structure comprising an introduction, a development and a conclusion. Each of these sections pursues its own communication objective and covers a certain amount of information.

Introduction	• Introduce the theme • Contextualise the subject (what is the reader's interest in the document)? • Where necessary, briefly present the documents studied • Lay out the framework
Development	Focused on the message itself, the development is structured in different sections in order to present information to the reader in a logical order and answer any questions they may have. It is made up of: • titles and sub-titles that coherently introduce the different information related to the subject • paragraphs, each introducing different and complementary elements
Conclusion	• Conclude the discussion and repeat the key information • An open-ended question (following the presentation of your ideas, asked directly of the reader about the subject, etc.)

Structural mistakes to avoid

- **Too much information is overkill.** Be sure to only convey the necessary information. For example, if you are writing an overview of the decisions taken at the last meeting, do not deviate from the agenda nor speak about future goals. Define an objective for the document and stick to it.
- **What is the subject?** It is difficult to avoid pronouns when writing: they lighten the text and save you from repeating yourself. However, note that their misuse could lose your reader's attention. Verify that, for each verb, the subject is clearly identifiable. Do not hesitate to

repeat it if you start a new paragraph, or you have raised another theme in the meantime.

- **Is layout an insignificant detail?** Definitely not! To hold the attention of your reader and allow them to digest all the information in your document, let them breathe. Nothing is more discouraging than a text without spaces, without line breaks, etc. Use the resources at your disposal to make your writing more attractive (layout, fonts, different typography).
- **Text, text and more text!** Sometimes an image speaks louder than words. You can also alternate between the two to energise your content. Consider all the possibilities you have (diagrams, sketches, tables, etc.), including writing summaries and minutes of meetings that are longer than usual.

Working on your style

In writing, form is as important as substance. The following tips will help you work and improve your style:

- **Read your text out loud.** Even if your document is in theory not intended to be read orally, this exercise will help you to perceive and improve where necessary the pace of your text and your writing style. Vary the tempo, use the appropriate words and use suitable punctuation, all of which will make for pleasant reading and retain the attention of your recipient.
- **Use the dictionary as often as possible.** Written communication is binding, due to the lack of direct contact with the reader. Therefore, words are the only medium for your message and you must measure the importance

of each in order to express your thoughts correctly. To find the right word, the use of a dictionary is required. This tool is not only useful for checking your spelling. Get into the habit of checking the meanings of terms and searching for synonyms and you will refine your vocabulary and find the right words for every situation.

- **Be concise.** Value quality over quantity. Sometimes we want to say too much, but long sentences often weigh down the text and undermine the reader's attention. Target the essential information, write in short sentences and look for the right words.
- **Practise.** Even though some people are more gifted than others, practice makes perfect. Therefore, it is by writing that you will become a better writer. Contrary to popular belief, style is not innate; it is acquired through work and training.

SOME SPECIFIC CASES

Some professional media are used more often than others. By following our advice, the drafting of these documents will soon be easy for you.

Professional e-mail

The e-mail is the primary means of communication in business, so it is essential to understand its formatting conventions:

The subject of your email Ensure that you are sufficiently clear and forceful, so that the reader immediately understands to what it refers.	"Room change for meeting on 24th September"
Greeting "Dear Sir" or "Dear Madam" is better than a simple informal "Hello". Add the surname of the person (or first name, if appropriate), in order to establish a link.	"Dear employees"
Content • Respect the introduction-development-conclusion structure so that the reader follows your train of thought. • Emphasise the key ideas of your message (put important information at the beginning of paragraphs, uses text forms such as italics and bold, bullet lists, etc.) • Pay attention to the length of your email: the longer it is, the less information will be retained. • Re-read your text in order to check its content and correct mistakes.	"The meeting on 24th September will no longer take place in the Orange room. We will all meet at 10am in the Violet room, which is located beside the cafeteria."
Conclusion • End your email will a polite salutation which is neither too familiar nor too formal. Opt for "Best wishes" or "Kind regards" if you know the recipient. • Finally, sign it: the signature transmits all the necessary information for your recipient to identify you and reply if needed (email, telephone, company role, etc.).	"I wish you all a good day. Best wishes, « Helena Lefas Administrative director Vent d'Hiver Email : helena.lefas@ ventdhiver.com Telephone : 02.50.86.78.36"

The business letter

The business letter is used to transmit messages to business partners or customers. Its aim is to convince, as well as to inform. It conveys the image of the company, so being as rigorous as possible runs the risk of your recipient running away. Use a neutral style that reveals the seriousness and efficiency of the company. The business letter usually takes the following form:

<table>
<tr><td>Header</td><td>First name and surname
Address
City and Postcode
Telephone and e-mail address</td></tr>
<tr><td></td><td align="right">Date</td></tr>
<tr><td></td><td><u>Subject</u> : the subject must be clear and draw in your reader.</td></tr>
<tr><td></td><td>Dear Sir/Madam, (delete as appropriate)</td></tr>
<tr><td>Introduction</td><td>Paragraph 1: In one or two sentences, explain why you are writing the letter.</td></tr>
<tr><td>Development</td><td>Paragraph 2: In this section, explain your arguments in order to convince the client or partner.</td></tr>
<tr><td>Conclusion</td><td>Paragraph 3: Summarise the decisions and your expectations.</td></tr>
<tr><td>Salutation</td><td>I hope that you will agree and I send you my highest regards.</td></tr>
<tr><td>Signature</td><td>H.L.</td></tr>
</table>

Minutes

Minutes are recorded in a document drafted after a meeting. This has two objectives:

- Summarise the discussion and keep a true and reliable record of the meeting's conclusions;
- Record the decisions and resulting actions.

The following advice will help you to draft it as well as possible:

Content	• The date, time and place of the meeting • The names of the participants and absentees • Different subjects and questions raised • Opinions expressed on each point • Decisions made and the actions to take • The name of employees who are in charge of their completion • The date, time, location and the subjects to tackle at the next meeting; • The signature of the meeting chairperson
Writing style	• The objective of minutes is to transcribe the comments made during the meeting as faithfully as possible: start by taking plenty of notes during the meeting in order to make the process easier when it comes to writing the report • Summarise what has been said, there is no need to write all the details • Write objectively and use the present tense • Finally, organise your writing chronologically or thematically

The memo and the briefing note

A memo (written by a superior to his employees) or briefing note is used to transmit a short message officially within the company. It includes the following information:

- **The recipient(s)** or the person to whom you are sending the text;
- **The sender**, i.e. the person who writes the note and

sends the information;

- **The date.** Write this without commas and with the year in full. You can also add a reference to the day of the week;
- **The subject.** As with e-mail, it must be forceful and clear to understand for the recipients;
- **The content.** Memos and briefing notes never open with 'Hello' or 'Dear Employee': get right to the heart of the matter. Be concise, your note should only deal with the information concerned;
- **The conclusion.** Finish with an acknowledgement;
- **Signature.** If you have already specified the name of the sender at the start, you can simply sign at the end of the note.

STAFF MEMO

Recipients: All members of staff

Sender: Helena Lefas, administrative director

Date: Tuesday 1st August 2015

<u>Subject</u>: Change of office door code

Following some security problems, we are required to change the access code for the office door. The new code will be in effect from 7th August 2015.

An email containing the new code will be sent to all members of staff. Keep an eye on your inbox.

Thank you for your understanding.

H.L.

TOP TIPS

- **Consider your reader:** if you want your text to be read, it must attract the interest of your reader. When planning and proofreading your writing, put yourself in the place of recipient. Also pay attention to the tone you are using: for example, if you are writing an e-mail to your boss or to a client, avoid slang.
- **Get to the point:** there is no need to provide a report that is ten pages long if the key information fits on three. The more you overload your document with details, the more inundated with information your reader will be and the less information they will retain. When you proofread, delete paragraphs, sentences or words that do not provide additional information or that seem superfluous.
- **Add examples:** theoretical information alone is often difficult to understand and take in. Examples will make your words more concrete and readers will better understand what you are referring to.
- **Write short sentences:** far from the style of Marcel Proust (1871-1922), a French writer famous for his endless sentences, effective writing is done through short sentences. During proofreading, when you think a sentence is too long to be understood easily, divide it into several sentences and highlight the main ideas.
- **Avoid banal words:** banish the verbs 'be', 'have' and 'do', which prevent you from qualifying your remarks. For example, opt for 'look' or 'sound' instead of 'be'; 'possess' or 'hold' instead of 'have'; 'bake' or 'simmer' instead of 'cook'. Similarly, the word 'thing' is banned!

- **Take your time:** the advantage of written communication is that you have time to think about the structure you want your message to have. Use your time wisely by being as specific as possible.
- **Avoid repetition:** although repeating the main information is essential for your reader to understand and retain it, excessive repetition of the same term or phrase should be avoided. Unlike oral communication, which often tends to use the same linking words ('you see', 'and so', 'and here', etc.), writing invites a wider variety of language tricks, otherwise you will run out of phrases.
- **Use the active voice:** besides weighing up formulations, passive voices give the impression that the subject is acted upon, rather than actions. Write 'We chose you as a new program designer', rather than 'You have been appointed as the designer of the new program', to emphasise the efforts and the receiver of the message.
- **Write in the present tense:** as many stories use the past tense when narrating, we feel that we have to follow this rule. In terms of communication, information narrated in the present tense has much more impact on the reader, as it appears as a current, known fact.
- **Highlight the logical connectors:** placing logical connectors at the beginning of paragraphs and phrases, such as 'since', 'however' or 'therefore' allow you to implicitly emphasise the structure of your presentation and mark the links between your ideas.
- **Choose affirmative sentences:** information within these sentences is more easily retained by the reader. For example, write "Store the records at the end of the meeting", instead of "Do not forget to store the records

at the end of the meeting".

FAQS

HOW CAN I FIGHT MY WRITER'S BLOCK?

You have all the elements to get you started in your writing: the subject is chosen and the necessary background research has been completed. You are ready to start writing, yet, when you put pen to paper, nothing comes out. The minutes pass and the frustration, anxiety, helplessness and even guilt intensify. To understand this phenomenon, try to analyse the causes. Véronique Mimeault (Canadian psychologist) identifies four:

- **Fear of failure.** Many people associate their professional performance with personal values. Sometimes we think that to exist we need to be professionally accomplished, and if we fail to perform a task entrusted to us, we need to re-evaluate our whole selves. In this context, the pressure is great when it comes to work. If we are putting our whole lives on the line every time we write, it is no surprise that we become worried whenever we have to do it. Therefore, relativize the situation and relax, for this exercise should not cause you anxiety. Try to think of it as more of a game.
- **Imposter syndrome.** A rite of passage for students and young workers early on in their career, undertaking written work for professors or superiors can be seen as an opportunity to potentially reveal their incompetence. This then becomes a fear of being unmasked. Diving into the deep end seems almost impossible.
- **Perfectionism.** By setting unrealistic goals and wanting

to write the perfect text in one draft, perfectionists may continue to contemplate their blank page instead of getting to work. Therefore, it is necessary to realise that a job is never done perfectly the first time. Accept that you will make mistakes: you will be able to rectify them with a second reading.

- **Self-censorship.** "They expect too much from my work", "My manager will not like it", etc. Anticipating negative reviews and feedback from readers before you have even started writing is certain to leave you stuck and unable to find words. Don't be so hard on yourself and give yourself a chance.

Fear of failing to do the job, being given a low mark, realising that the text will never be perfect, or receiving criticism from peers and superiors will get you nowhere. Instead of second-guessing what could happen, start to trust yourself and believe in your abilities.

WHAT TYPES OF WRITTEN COMMUNICATION ARE FOUND IN BUSINESS?

In the professional world, it is necessary to distinguish between internal and external communication. Indeed, you will use different media in each of the two circumstances. The following table lists the types of professional writing that you can find for each type of communication:

Internal communication	External communication
• Email	• Email
• Staff memo	• Brochure, prospectus
• Meeting minutes, reports	• Press release
• Summary	• Commercial letter
• Company newsletter	• Newsletter
• Etc.	• Etc.

HOW CAN I DEFINE THE PURPOSE OF MY TEXT?

Any professional document intends to transmit a message. To achieve this goal, you must have a clear concept of the idea you want to communicate and its terms. Therefore, ask yourself the following questions:

- What information am I sending?
- To whom?
- Why?

These answers will help you to identify if the text is informative, argumentative or has another purpose. Only then can you choose a suitable medium. In both cases, summarise the purpose of your text with a tagline or catchy title: your reader will immediately understand what type of communication it is and take an interest.

HOW CAN I ENSURE MY DOCUMENT CONTAINS ALL THE NECESSARY INFORMATION?

To ensure you do not miss any crucial information, make sure that the following questions can be answered:

- What?
- Who?
- When?
- How?
- Where?
- Why?

Did you answer all these questions?

HOW DO I FORMULATE AN ARGUMENT?

GLOSSARY

- Opinion: personal judgment.
- Fact: proven, real.
- Argument: opinion which is based on fact. It aims to convince the reader to agree with our personal opinion.

To convince the reader, you must prove what you are saying and construct the text to do this. There are several tools that you can use to attest the veracity of your statements.

Types of arguments	Example
Definition	"Of course we should ban bullfighting. How can we allow these spectacles to continue when they lead to the death of an innocent animal?"
Comparison	"Is it better to condone factory farming, with animals ending up dying in an abattoir, than to allow them to live in dignity, in open air, and die in an arena?" "The problem with debates on bullfighting is that the majority of its opponents do not know what is involved in the practice and base their views on videos and gory images. This is exactly like me showing images of children crying in a playground and saying: "Look how cruel school is!""
Cause and effect link	"Banning bullfighting would be a mistake, as if it disappeared, the Corbas bull race would die with it."
Quote from expert or authoritative document on the subject	"The law itself recognises violence against animals as an act of cruelty."

By relying on a specific item, you will be more objective and legitimate in your personal opinion. For example, you may want to establish additional hours as part of your training: remind your audience that entering a trade without having enough experience in the field is like learning to swim on a stool (argument by comparison). Or, you may want to plan a relaxation area for your team in your workplace, basing your argument on the well-founded benefits of this practice (argument of authority).

HOW CAN I HIGHLIGHT THE KEY IDEAS OF MY TEXT?

- Drafting a clear and concise title that exposes the main topic of your document and its challenges.
- Organising your text with chapters and subtitles that reflect the secondary ideas discussed in the text.
- Introducing each key point at the beginning of a paragraph.
- Using different types of characters to highlight keywords (bold, italic, underline, etc.).
- Repeating key information in the form of a bulleted list at the beginning or end of your document.

WHY SHOULD I BE CONCISE IN MY WRITING AND HOW IS THIS DONE?

Being able to speak and be understood in just a few words is an art. To ensure the conciseness of your text, some rules apply:

- **Remove superfluous text.** Avoid adding information that is not directly related to your main subject. Anything that does not contribute to the understanding of the message should be deleted.
- **Remove as many adverbs as possible,** as many of them are useless.
- **Avoid phrases that add nothing to the clarity of the message.** For example: "(It goes without saying that) your presence at the meeting is necessary".
- **Play with punctuation.** The colon can sometimes

replace the conjunction 'because'. So, the phrase "The project was not successful: we did not have the supplies in time" will have more impact on the reader. A semi-colon can replace a conjunction of contrast in a mirror structure, for example in the sentence "The teacher's role is to educate; the students' is to learn".
- **Use precise words.** Replace nominal phrases with single words. For example, 'in recent times' with 'recently'.
- **Rephrase long sentences.** Divide them into several shorter sentences. In doing so, the sentence "For this program, which is important for the company to be successful with our IT customers, we must adapt to the needs of their profession" will become "This program is important for the company. To be a hit with our IT customers, we must adapt to the needs of their profession".

WHAT REFERENCE TOOLS ARE USED FOR WRITING?

- An English dictionary (such as the Oxford English Dictionary) to check precise definitions
- A grammar reference book
- A thesaurus

HOW CAN I EFFECTIVELY PROOFREAD MY DOCUMENT?

Self-correcting

- If you have time, leave a period of time between writing and proofreading. If you rework your document after one or two days, you will have a clear head and be able to take a step back in order to spot faults and mistakes.

- After a first proofreading on your computer, print your document to read it on paper. While this technique may seem archaic in the computer age, changing media will help you to concentrate and design your text differently.
- For consistent and effective checking, carry out your proofreading in separate sections, to reduce the risk of overlooking any passages in the text.
- Proofread three times:
  - A first, to check the background and accuracy of the information.
  - A second, to ensure the overall coherence and structure of the text;
  - A third, to check spelling and grammar.

Asking another person

This is the ideal solution if you have the means to do so, or if someone you know is prepared to help you. You can turn to three types of readers:

- A non-expert proof-reader who knows nothing about the subject matter and serves as a kind of 'typical reader'. They can tell you if the information is set out sufficiently in order to be understood by the average person;
- An expert proof-reader who has a good understanding of the subject and will help to verify the accuracy of your data;
- A 'grammar police' proof-reader, to make the final spelling and grammar checks of your text.

OVER TO YOU!

CHECKLIST FOR EFFECTIVE WRITING

To perform a self-assessment, answer the following questions:

Introduction

Have I achieved the goals of my introduction?

- Have I written an attention-grabbing first sentence to contextualise the theme of my text?
- Have I briefly announced the structure of the text and how the elements are arranged within it?

Have I respected the constraints of an introduction?

- Have I assumed that the reader knows nothing about the subject?
- Is the introduction suitably short (ideally, not exceeding 1/7th of the text)?

Development

- Is the structure of my text clear?
- Have I divided the text into coherent paragraphs (one paragraph = one idea)?

Conclusion

Have I concluded my document by highlighting the main ideas?

NOTES TO REMEMBER

Practise writing sentences using the following connectors:

Setting out your points	Firstly, secondly, etc. In the first place, etc. To begin, then, finally, etc. On the one hand, on the other hand, etc.
Adding ideas	Then, furthermore, moreover, etc.
Marking an opposition or concession	Although, however, nonetheless, despite, etc.
Marking a link	Because, given that, under the pretext that, since, etc.
Indicating a consequence	Thus, therefore, consequently, etc.
Summarising, concluding comments	In conclusion, to summarise, in the end, etc.

REFORMULATION EXERCISES

There is nothing like a little practice to improve. Rephrase the following sentences to make them understandable and more enjoyable to read. Remember that the reader must clearly identify the subject of each verb and the idea you want to convey.

- "If you do not want your baby to get sick, you must use clean bottles; when he is finished, open the bottle and place all parts in a sterilizer."
- "Despite previous disagreements between the different participants, we have reached the end of the negotiations and achieved a settlement that includes the key points raised by both the parents' association and the board of

directors and should be implemented as early as the next school year."
- "I met Mr. Smith's partner, who was about to send an e-mail to the Head teacher regarding the behaviour of the maths teacher towards their son, and who told me that he would not be seeing him again."
- "According to him, the victim died about 18 hours ago."
- "The inspector was investigating the death of the corrupt president when he discovered his missing body under the floorboards: it was rotten."
- Doctor: "Then you take me for a man who would do anything for money, for a man fond of money, for a mercenary soul? Know, my friend, that if you were to give me a purse full of gold, and that this purse were in a rich box, this box in a precious case, this case in a superb chest, this chest in a rare museum, this museum in a magnificent apartment, this apartment in a gorgeous castle, this castle in a wonderful citadel, this citadel in a celebrated town, this town in a fertile island, this island in an opulent province, this province in a flourishing monarchy, this monarchy in the whole world; that if you gave me the world in which this flourishing monarchy would be, in which this opulent province would be, in which this fertile island would be, in which this celebrated town would be, in which this wonderful citadel would be, in which this gorgeous castle would be, in which this pleasant apartment would be, in which this rare museum would be, in which this wonderful chest would be, in which this precious case would be, in which this rich box would be, in which the purse full of gold would be, I should care no more for it than this." (Molière, *The Jealousy of Le Barbouillé*, Act I, Scene II)

We want to hear from you!
Leave a comment on your online library
and share your favourite books on social media!

FURTHER READING

BIBLIOGRAPHY

- BFM TV. (2012) *Faut- il interdire la corrida ?* [Online]. [Accessed 7 August 2015]. Available from: <https://www.youtube.com/watch?v=HChfbT3aGQ4>
- Bien écrire. (No date) *La lettre commerciale.* [Online]. [Accessed 21 August 2015]. Available from: <http://www.bienecrire.org/lettre-commerciale.php>
- Bourget, M. (No date) La note et la note de service. Modèles. *Visez juste en français.* [Online]. [Accessed 21 August 2015]. Available from: <http://www.visezjuste.uottawa.ca/pages/redaction/note_de_service_modele.html>
- Colson, J. (1987) *Le dissertoire. De l'art de raisonner et de rédiger.* Brussels: De Boeck.
- Girard, B. (1997) *La communication écrite dans l'entreprise.* Brussels: De Boeck.
- Griselein, M., Carpentier, C., Maïllarde, J., and Ormaux, S. (1992) *Guide de la communication écrite.* Paris: Dunod.
- Maccio, C. (1992) *Savoir écrire un livre... un rapport... un mémoire. De la pensée à l'écriture.* Lyon: Chronique sociale, coll. "L'essentiel".
- Meunier, J. and Peraya, D. (1993) *Introduction aux théories de la communication.* Brussels: De Boeck.
- Mimeault, V. (No date) L'étape de la rédaction. Surmonter le phénomène de la page blanche. *Centre d'aide aux étudiants de l'université de Laval.* [Online]. [Accessed 17 August 2015]. Available from: <https://www.aide.ulaval.ca/cms/Accueil/

Apprentissage_et_Reussite/2e_3e_cycles/Page_blanche>
- Niquet, G. (1983) *Écrire avec logique et clarté*. No 31. Paris: Hatier.
- Oury, P. (1990) *Rédiger pour être lu. Les secrets de la communication écrite efficace*. Brussels: De Boeck.
- Peyroutet, C. (2002) *Style et rhétorique*. Paris: Nathan, coll. "Repères pratiques".
- Peyroutet, C. (2005) *La pratique de l'expression écrite*. Paris: Nathan, coll. "Repères pratiques".
- Richaudeau, F. (1984) *Le langage efficace*, Paris: Retz.

ADDITIONAL SOURCES

- BtB. (No date) *La langue claire et simple.* [Online]. [Accessed 21 August 2015]. Available from http://www. btb.termiumplus.gc.ca/redac-chap?lang=fra&lettr =chapsect10&info0=10
- Vallée, C. (No date) Les règles générales de la communication écrite. *École supérieure de l'éducation nationale.* [Online]. [Accessed 7 August 2015]. Available from: <http://www.esen.education.fr/fileadmin/user_upload/ Modules/Ressources/Outils/communicatioc_inspecteur/ vallee_c_regles_comm_ecrite_2.pdf>

www.50minutes.com

Ebook EAN: 9782806279385

Paperback EAN: 9782806284310

Legal Deposit: D/2016/12603/377

Cover: © Primento

Digital conception by Primento, the digital partner of publishers.

Made in the USA
Monee, IL
07 July 2026